Avia Bk-534, 13th Squadron, Slovak Air Force, Eastern Front, Kiev sector, 1942. Colour scheme as for B6.

CZECHOSLOVAKIAN AIR FORCE 1918-1970

Text by Zdenek Titz

Illustrated by Gordon C. Davies and Richard Ward

Compiled by Zdenek Titz

ACKNOWLEDGEMENTS

We would like to thank the many friends without whose help this survey of the Czechoslovakian Air Force would not have been possible. They are in alphabetical order:

Joe Benesh, Miroslav Fiala, Frank Fort, Oldřich Kožušníček, B. Ladalkan, Ludvik Michalec, Ladislav Valoušek.

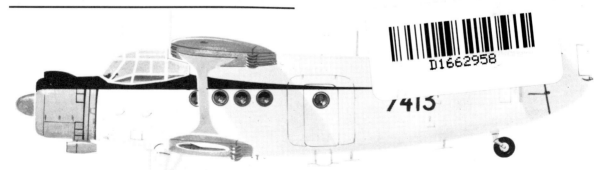

Antanov An-2, multi-purpose aircraft used mostly for parachute troop training. Fuselage, fin and rudder cream, engine cowl, wings and tail-plane blue/grey, spinner red, top of engine cowl and cheat line black.

Published by: Osprey Publications Limited, England

Editorial Office: P.O. Box 5, Canterbury, Kent, England

Subscription & Business Office: P.O. Box 25, 707 Oxford Road, Reading, Berkshire, England

The Berkshire Printing Co. Ltd. © Osprey Publications Ltd. 1971   SBN 85045 021 7   Not for sale in U.S.A.

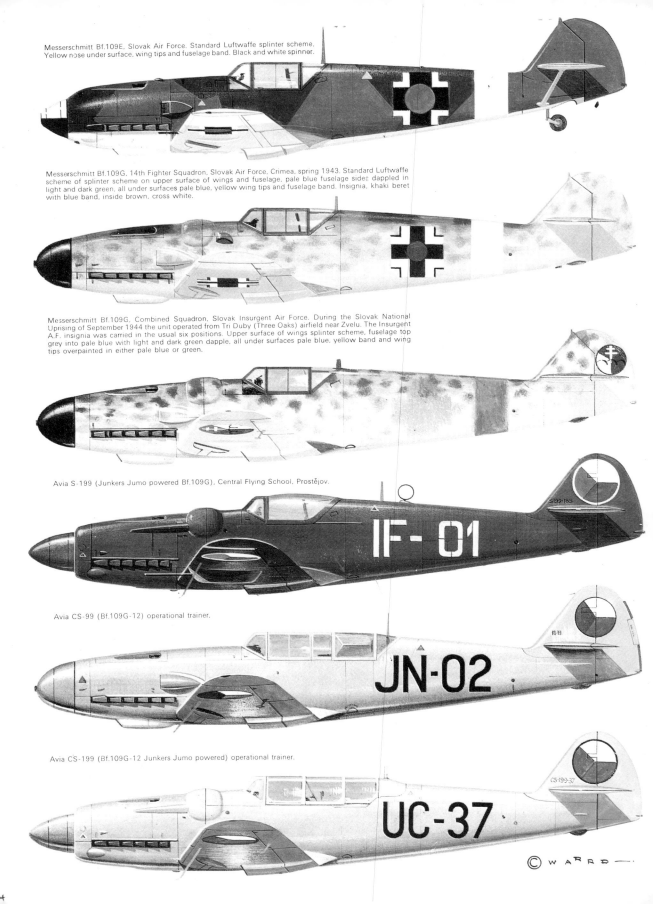

Messerschmitt Bf.109E, Slovak Air Force. Standard Luftwaffe splinter scheme. Yellow nose under surface, wing tips and fuselage band. Black and white spinner.

Messerschmitt Bf.109G, 14th Fighter Squadron, Slovak Air Force, Crimea, spring 1943. Standard Luftwaffe scheme of splinter scheme on upper surface of wings and fuselage, pale blue fuselage sides dappled in light and dark green, all under surfaces pale blue, yellow wing tips and fuselage band. Insignia, khaki beret with blue band, inside brown, cross white.

Messerschmitt Bf.109G, Combined Squadron, Slovak Insurgent Air Force. During the Slovak National Uprising of September 1944 the unit operated from Tri Duby (Three Oaks) airfield near Zvelu. The Insurgent A.F. insignia was carried in the usual six positions. Upper surface of wings splinter scheme, fuselage top grey into pale blue with light and dark green dapple, all under surfaces pale blue, yellow band and wing tips overpainted in either pale blue or green.

Avia S-199 (Junkers Jumo powered Bf.109G), Central Flying School, Prostějov.

Avia CS-99 (Bf.109G-12) operational trainer.

Avia CS-199 (Bf.109G-12 Junkers Jumo powered) operational trainer.

4

Line-up of Avia B-534 biplane fighters of the fourth production series with enclosed cockpit prior to delivery to squadrons.

CZECHOSLOVAKIAN AIR FORCE 1918-1970

The birth of the Czechoslovak armed forces occurred simultaneously with the founding of the independent Czechoslovak state on 28 October 1918. Up to this date the areas of Bohemia, Moravia and Slovakia were parts of the Austro-Hungarian Empire; many personnel of Czech origin served with the Imperial Air Service, but there were no national air units. Most of these personnel served as ground crewmen, and only a score or two managed to become pilots; but during the First World War individual Czechs or small groups had served as members of Czech Legions with the air services of France and Russia.

The first Czechoslovak Air Force unit was formed on 9 June 1918 in Russia, under the designation *Čs. letecky oddil čs. legii v Rusku*—"Czechoslovak Air Division of Cz. Legions in Russia". The unit, first commanded by F/O Melč, began operations with only two aircraft, a Farman 30 and a Voisin 2. Shortly thereafter a second Air Division was formed under the command of Captain Fiala. The activities of both divisions were limited to reconnaissance flights. In April 1919 the 1st Division was re-organised as a flying school at Omsk, with 170 personnel; on 2 June the school received seven American "Tractor" aircraft, and commenced flying training. The establishment at Omsk was only transferred to the newly-founded Czechoslovak Republic in 1920.

In the meanwhile, the *Čs. letecky sbor*—"Czechoslovak Air Corps"—had been founded in Prague. The first aircraft were machines confiscated on the airfield of Cheb in Western Bohemia, the only properly-constructed airfield on Bohemian or Moravian territory. These Imperial machines were mainly Brandenburg biplanes, and were transported by air and road to Prague, where a new airfield was quickly prepared and named Prague/Kbely. This field became the base for the 1st Squadron, which immediately commenced flying training with the Brandenburg biplanes. During 1919 the first 20 pilots completed their training.

During 1919 and 1920 the Cz.A.F. received 128 aircraft from France, including 50 SPAD VII and SPAD XIII scouts; 50 Salmson 2 reconnaissance biplanes; 15 Voisin 8, ten Breguet 14 and one Liore et Olivier 7/2 bombers; and two Farman Goliaths. With the expropriated aircraft

(which included such types as the Brandenburg C.1, the Fokker D.VII, the Albatros D.II, the Nieuport 11, and various Ansaldo, Roland and Phönix machines) the total equipment in 1920 reached 165 aircraft. This total was divided among 11 squadrons, formed one by one over the next two years. By late 1922 four fighter and seven reconnaissance squadrons had been formed; the young air force continued to increase, and in 1923 three Air Regiments were formed. Each regiment consisted of two *letecky prapor* (loosely, Wing or Group, but there is no exact English translation); and each *letecky prapor* was made up of three squadrons. The 1st Air Regiment was based at Prague (Bohemia), the 2nd at Olomouc (Moravia), and the 3rd at Nitra (Slovakia). Simultaneously, and under the direct control of the Ministry of National Defence, the independent *Letecky sbor* (Air Division) and *Letecky studijni ústav* (Air Research Institute) were founded, and a chain of meteorological stations set up.

In 1923 the organisation of the Air Regiment included: H.Q., I and II *letecky prapor* (later, I and II *perut*, balloon squadron, photographic unit, reserve squadron, regimental workshops, and regimental stores. Each *perut* consisted of three squadrons. During the same year the *Letecky dopravni oddil* (Air Transport Division) was established and began a regular air line service on the route Prague-Bratislava-Košice. This Division, in fact, laid the basis for the later Č.S.A. Company. During 1924 Cheb airfield became the site for the *Škola leteckého dorostu* (Advanced Flying School) and the building of the *Vojenská továrna na letadla* (Military Aircraft Factory), later contracted to Letov, was nearing completion. Here, the first Czech military aircraft was designed and built; designated Letnov Šm-1, it was a reconnaissance biplane of Alois Šmolik design.

Operational flight training was provided by the Reserve Squadrons attached to each regimental establishment. The central flying school, or *Letecké učiliste*, was completed at Prostejov in Moravia in 1925, and took over the training of most Czech aircrew and ground personnel. During the first ten years of the Air Force's existence nine airfields were built: these were Prague/Kbely, Milovice, Olomouc, Prostejov, Brno, Piešťany, Bratislava, Nitra, and Košice. Additionally, several auxiliary airstrips were available to

Spad S-XIII, showing the original roundel of the Cz.A.F., on Olomouc airfield, Moravia, 1922.

the Air Force in various parts of the country.

For the first few years the Air Force was naturally obliged to use aircraft of foreign origin, but an effort was made to replace them with indigenous types as soon as this became possible. The three main aircraft factories were Letov, Avia and Aero. The Letov plant was originally controlled directly by the Ministry of National Defence, but in 1936 became a civil factory. In 1925 design and production work also started at the famous Škoda plant at Pilsen, which acquired a licence to build the Dewoitine D-1 fighter. The replacement of obsolete foreign types with Czech designs began in 1921 with the Letov Šm-1; in 1923 about 45 per cent, and over the next five years about 90 per cent, of aircraft in service were of Czech design. By 1928 Czech manufacturers were able to offer 50 different designs, 34 of them in series production.

In 1928 the Air Force consisted of 23 field squadrons, ten of them fighter, ten reconnaissance, and three bomber squadrons. The 4th Air Regt. was established in the same year, followed in 1929 by the 6th and in 1930 by the 5th. The 4th Air Regt. and the 6th Air Regt. together formed the *Letecká brigáda* (Air Brigade) based at Prague. The peacetime establishment of the Air Force was reached in 1931, and represented the main force of the Cz.A.F. until the mobilisation of 1938.

The designation of squadrons by consecutive numerals, irrespective of the parent regiment, was followed throughout; Nos. 1-30 were observer squadrons, 31-50 light fighter squadrons, 51-60 heavy fighter squadrons, 61-70 reconnaissance squadrons, 71-80 light bomber squadrons, 81-90 heavy bomber squadrons, and 91 and above, night fighter squadrons. The allocation of squadrons to regiments was as follows:

1st Air Regt. (Mixed) "President T. G. Masaryk", based at Prague.
Observer and Reconnaissance Sqns. 1, 2, 3, 4, 6, 11, 61, 66.
Fighter Sqns. 31, 32, 34.

2nd Air Regt. (Mixed) "Dr Edward Benes", based at Olomouc.
Observer and Reconnaissance Sqns. 5, 7, 8, 14, 62, 63.
Fighter Sqns. 33, 35, 36, 51.
Night Fighter Sqn. 91.

3rd Air Regt. (Mixed) "General M. R. Stefánik", based Piešťany.
Observer and Reconnaissance Sqns. 9, 10, 12, 13, 15, 16, 64.
Fighter Sqns. 37, 38, 39, 45, 49.

4th Air Regt. (Fighter), based at Hradec Králové.
Fighter Sqns. 40, 41, 42, 43, 44, 46, 47, 48, 50.

5th Air Regt. (Bomber), based at Brno.
Bomber Sqns. 75, 76, 77, 81, 82, 83, 84.

6th Air Regt. (Bomber), based at Prague and Milovice.
Bomber Sqns. 71, 72, 73, 74.

Bomber and reconnaissance squadrons consisted of three flights each, fighter squadrons of four flights.

The strength of the Cz.A.F. during the Munich crisis of 1938 was as follows: 16 Observer Squadrons with 160 aircraft, 21 Fighter Squadrons with 252 aircraft, five Reconnaissance Squadrons with 50 aircraft, 11 Bomber Squadrons with 94 aircraft, one Night Fighter Squadron with ten aircraft. The total first-line strength was thus 566 aircraft. The total number of aircraft available, including Reserve Squadrons and machines of other categories, on 1 September 1938 was 1,514, comprising:

529 observer aircraft
61 reconnaissance aircraft
326 fighters
101 light bombers
54 heavy bombers
207 trainers
399 advanced trainers
107 liaison aircraft.

During the dramatic days of March 1939, when Bohemia and Moravia were occupied by the Germans, the complete equipment of the Cz.A.F. was confiscated by the *Luftwaffe* without opposition. To this enormous booty were added the aircraft of civil aero clubs and both airlines, Č.S.A. and Č.L.S. Most of these Czech aircraft were used by the *Luftwaffe* for training purposes, but others were made available for sale to German satellite states. The Bulgarian Air Force received 48 Avia B-534 fighters, 12 Avia B-122, 30 Letov Š-328, 42 Avia B-71(SB-2), 12 Avia B-135, six Bloch MB-200 and a few Aero A-304. A number of aircraft also went to Hungary and Slovakia. Czech aircraft factories in the so-called "Protectorate of Bohemia-Moravia" were forced to start production of German types.

Following the rape of their country and the demobilisation of their Air Force, large numbers of Cz.A.F. personnel escaped across the borders of the "Protectorate" by various routes, and began their long and eventful search for opportunities to fight against the occupiers of their homeland. Most of them reached Poland, where they tended to be concentrated around Krakow. Shortly before the invasion of Poland by Germany, 477 Czech airmen left Polish harbours in five ships bound for France. Initially they were forced to serve in the French Foreign Legion; however, when Germany attacked France they were transferred into the French *Armée de l'Air*. Plans were in hand to form separate units of Czech pilots, but the French capitulation came too soon for these plans to reach fruition, and the Ccech pilots were scattered throughout many French *Groupes de Chasse* during the Battle of France, including the famous *Cigognes*. During the campaign Czechs claimed the destruction of 147 enemy aircraft confirmed and 19 probables. After the collapse in France, they escaped by many different routes to their next "station"—England.

The Czech airmen were warmly welcomed in England and immediately offered their services in the defence of the country. By 15 August 1940, 906 Cz.A.F. personnel had reached Britain, and this figure increased to 1,287 before the end of the year. On 12 July 1940 No. 310 (Czech) Fighter Squadron was raised at Duxford, becoming operational on 18 August. This was followed by No. 311 (Czech) Bomber Squadron on 2 August, No. 312 (Czech) Fighter Squadron on 5 September, and on 5 May 1941, by No. 313 (Czech) Fighter Squadron. The flying and operational training of Czech personnel was carried out in British flying schools and O.T.U.s, and in Canada and the Bahamas. Apart from the all-Czech units, a number of Czechs served with British squadrons, including Nos. 19 and 68. A Czech sergeant, Josef František, flew with the Polish No. 303 Squadron during September 1940, and became the top Allied fighter pilot of the Battle of Britain, with 17 confirmed solo victories in the space of 28 days. He was killed in action on 8 October. Shortly before D-Day the three Czech fighter squadrons were brought together in the Czech Fighter Wing, which operated as part of the 2nd Tactical Air Force. Between August 1940 and 1 January 1945, Czech airmen flying with the Royal Air Force recorded 326 victories; during the same period 506 Czech airmen were lost.

The Czechoslovak Air Force in exile also took part in the fight against the *Luftwaffe* and *Wehrmacht* on the Eastern Front. On 19 February 1944 the ship *Reina del Pacifico* left England for the Soviet Union, carrying 21 Czech veterans of R.A.F. squadrons to become the nucleus of the Czechoslovak units in the East. Their first base was Ivanovo, where they trained on the Russian Lavochkin La-5 fighter, an easy task for former Hurricane and Spitfire pilots. Operational training commenced soon afterwards, to master the rather different tactics of Russian fighter squadrons. On 7 May 1944 the group moved to Kubinka airfield near Moscow, and was joined by groundcrew personnel, then officially becoming the 128th Independent Fighter Squadron, ready to go into

action on the Russo-German front. Meanwhile the Soviet Union had decided to form an independent Czechoslovak Fighter Regiment within the framework of the Soviet Air Force; this regiment was to consist of the 128th Squadron and two others, personnel being drawn from those already under training in Russian flying schools and from those who had fled from the so-called Slovak State, which was a German puppet regime. Wing Commander František Fajtl, an experienced R.A.F. fighter pilot, was nominated as commander of the 1st Czechoslovak Fighter Regiment.

The great news of the D-Day landings in France reached the Czech and Slovak pilots just as they were preparing to go into action; the regimental commander sought permission from the Red Army to commence operations immediately, and his request was granted. On 20 July 1944 two squadrons of La-5FN fighters moved up to the forward airfield of Proskurov, near Lwow, and it was here that the pilots heard the unexpected news of the Slovak National Uprising. They naturally expressed a wish to go and assist their compatriots, and between 7 and 11 September the regiment transferred to Stubno airfield in Poland, close to the front line.

In Slovakia, where a puppet government had been set up to collaborate with Hitler, the opposition of Czechs and Slovaks had passed from clandestine partisan activities into open warfare. The centre of the uprising was the town of Banská Bystrica. At the beginning the leader of the insurgent forces, General Golian, had at his disposal only a weak and obsolete air force, based on the airfields if Tri Duby (Three Oaks) and Zolná. Initially 57 machines were available for use: three Avia B-534, two Bf. 109E, two Bf 109G, three Letov Š-328, two S.M.84bis, two Ju 52/3m, one Fw 189, two Fw 58, two Ju W.34, 30 Fw 44 and He 72, six Praga E-39, and two Klemm Kl 35D. This motley assortment formed the equipment of the so-called "Combined Squadron", which went into

Above: Line-up of Spad S-XIII's of the flying school at Cheb, West Bohemia 1921.

Below: Hansa-Brandenburg C-1 with Hiero 230h.p. engine, the camouflage indicates the period 1923–1926.

Above: Aero A-18's of the first delivery batch with Spads in the distance.

Above: Aero A-18, 2nd Air Regiment after a crash landing on Olomouc airfield in 1925. Note the regimental insignia.
Below: Aero A-18 fighter biplane with BMW IIIa 185h.p. engine, 1st Air Regiment, Kbely airfield, Prague 1923. Twenty A-18's were delivered to the Cz.A.F.

Above: Avia BH-3 fighter of 1921 powered by a Walter W-IV engine of 220h.p. Ten aircraft only of this type were delivered.

Below: Avia BH-4 prototype with Hispano Suiza 8 Ba engine of 220h.p. on the Prague-Letnany airfield.

Below: Avia BH-10 designed and built for aerobatic training, first flown in 1924 with Walter NZ 60h.p., engine. Central Flying School, Prostejov, Moravia.

A Hansa-Brandenburg C-1 flown by Frantisek Divis on its nose on an unknown airfield some time in 1925.

action immediately; but to pit such machines against the modern equipment of the *Luftwaffe* was hopeless. Then, on 17 Sepember 1944, the insurgent air force received its most significant reinforcement; from the Polish airfield of Krosno 21 Lavochkin La-5FN fighters flew in to Zolná. The original rôle of the fighter regiment had been changed to the direct support of the insurgent ground forces; and the first operation was a low-level attack on the air base at Piešťany. Unfortunately the landing of the fighter regiment behind enemy lines in Slovakia occurred at a time when the National Uprising was already on the defensive; and on 24 October H.Q. decided to interrupt operations and ordered the ground troops and air force groundcrew to move into the mountains and continue the struggle from more secure bases. At 13.45 hrs. on 25 October the first Lavochins took off and set course for the liberated Hungarian airfield of Przeworsk. The activities of the 1st Czechoslovak Fighter Regiment were notable from a historical point of view, for in no other European theatre of operations during the Second World War did a comparable unit operate from behind enemy lines.

Late in October 1944 the Soviet authorities agreed to the establishment of the 2nd Czechoslovak Air Regiment (La-5FN) and the 3rd Czechoslovak Assault Regiment (I1-2). Each regiment consisted of three squadrons; and together these three regiments formed the 1st Czechoslovak Mixed Division, which operated within the framework of the 8th Soviet Air Army. The Divisional Commander was Colonel L. Budin; the division became operational on 14 April 1945 and took part in the fighting around Ostrava and Opava in Northern Moravia, flying La-5FN and La-7 fighters and I1-2 ground-attack aircraft.

The Slovak Air Force

The history of the air force of the so-called Slovak State is a separate but parallel story. After the occupation of Bohemia and Moravia in March 1939, the Germans dissolved the Czechoslovak Republic and declared Slovakia an autonomous state; and a small Slovak air arm was promptly established under *Luftwaffe* patronage.

This comprised one regiment made up of six combat flights and a training squadron. The equipment was largely of obsolete pre-war Czech origin, such as Avia B-534 fighter biplanes, Letov Š-328 reconnaissance aircraft, and Aero A-100 light bombers.

In July 1939 the Slovak President Tiso agreed to *Luftwaffe* bomber units moving on to the Slovak airfields of Spišská Nová Ves and Piešťany in preparation for the attack on Poland; and when this campaign opened Slovak A.F. units made a few desultory attacks on Polish targets in support of the *Luftwaffe*, including a bombing raid on Tarnopol. The combination of obsolete aircraft and a total lack of enthusiasm on the part of the Slovak aircrews produced predictably unimpressive results. By the close of 1940 the Slovak A.F. comprised three fighter squadrons (Nos. 11 and 13 at Piešťany and No. 12 at Spišská Nová Ves); three reconnaissance squadrons (Nos. 1, 2 and 3, based at Zilina, Spišská Nová Ves and Nitra); a technical wing, and a reserve wing. In November 1941 a contingent of the S1.A.E. was transferred to the Russian Front. Naturally enough, the Avia B-534s and Letovs proved incapable of operating effectively under winter conditions, and after a time they were returned to Slovakia. The fighting record of the Avias in the Kiev sector was hardly impressive, and only one pilot was lost; he deserted to the Russians with his aircraft.

By 1942 the equipment of the S1.A.F. was in dire need of replacement, and 30 Klemm Kl 35D, 30 Focke-Wulf Fw 44, 30 Gotha Go 145 and six Arado Ar 96B trainers were acquired, together with ten Caudron C.445 Goeland crew trainers. New operational equipment also delivered at this time comprised ten Savoia Marchetti S.M.84bis, 14 Focke-Wulf Fw 189, ten Fieseler Fi 156C, two Heinkel He 111, and 14 Messerschmitt Bf 109E fighters. For transport duties, two Ju 52/3m and six Ju W.34 were acquired. In 1943 the 12th Fighter Squadron became operational with Bf 109Es on the southern sector of the Russian Front, moving as far forward as Maicop in the Causasus. The unit subsequently lost all its aircraft in the later retreat, due to an inexplicable shortage of fuel which came to light when the squadron was ordered to vacate

Anatra DS powered by a 150h.p., Salmson-Canton-Unne nine-cylinder water-cooled radial engine, Olomouc airfield, 1920.

its base . . . The squadron was re-equipped in due course with new Bf 109G fighters, providing air cover for the so-called "Slovak Fast Division" in the Crimea. By this time unit morale had reached rock bottom, and little sympathy remained for the Slovak Government or their German masters. Although Dr. Goebbels claimed that Slovak pilots had shot down 154 enemy aircraft on the Russian Front, they had in fact avoided combat whenever possible, reported fictitious "kills", and put 27 Messerschmitts out of action through deliberate mishandling. Many Slovak crews deserted to the Russians with their aircraft. For example, on 18 April 1943 the crew of the one and only Avia B-71 (SB-2) in the S1.A.F. succeeded in stealing the aircraft and flying ,without incident, to Turkey; they later reached Egypt and subsequently arrived in England to join a Czechoslovak squadron.

In 1943 No. 3 Reconnaissance Squadron was transferred to the Crimea, where it retrained on the He 111. The S1.A.F. now consisted of some 4,000 personnel divided between fighter, bomber and reconnaissance squadrons, the flying school at Zvolen, the depot at Mokrad and the A.F.H.Q. at Trenčin. The Air Force was commanded by General S. Jurech, and at the peak of its strength never possessed more than 78 first line aircraft. By early in 1944 defections by personnel were reaching alarming proportions; and when the National Uprising began on 29 August, 38 Slovak aircraft, carrying 108 personnel, promptly crossed the lines and landed at Soviet airfields, while others concentrated at Tri Duby and began attacking German forces. After the uprising, the Slovak Air Force was never revived.

The Czechoslovak Air Force Post-War

Although large numbers of German aircraft were left behind on Bohemian and Moravian airfields at the time of the Czechoslovak liberation in May 1945, many had been damaged or destroyed by surrendering German troops, and only a few were available for use. The Czech factories—Avia, Letov, Aero, Zlin, etc.—were immediately faced with the task of switching from production of German types and beginning to re-equip the Cz.A.F. The nucleus of the aircraft park was provided by those machines brought home by Czechoslovak units from England and the Soviet Union. These comprised 76 Spitfire L.F.IXE, 26 Mosquito F.B.VI, about 40 Lavochkin La-5FN, La-7 and La-5UTI, about 20 Ilyushin I1-2, and a few Petiyakov Pe-2, Po-2, Avro Anson, Airspeed Oxford, WACO CG-4A, etc. Naturally, these aircraft were insufficient for the needs of a whole air force; salvaged German types were pressed into service, and in some cases production of German designs were continued in Czech factories as a temporary expedient. The Aero plant completed a series of 260 Bückner Bü 131 biplanes for elementary training and the Zlin factory produced some 180 Bü 181s for the same purpose. Avia and Aero delivered 394 Arado Ar 96Bs, and the latter factory, in collaboration with ČKD-Praga, completed 179 Siebel Fh 204Ds for both the Air Force and the airline Č.S.A. The Mraz factory in Chocen completed a batch of 138 Fieseler Fi 156 Storch general duty light aircraft; but the most significant production series was the batch of re-worked Bf 109G fighters produced by Avia.

Some hundreds of Bf 109 airframes were concentrated in Prague from all over the country. There was a shortage of the original DB 605 engines, but fortunately good stocks of Junkers Jumo 211F powerplants remained. Avia re-worked the basic Bf 109G-6 to take the Jumo engine, and designated the result the S-199; a two-seat version was also produced under the designation CS-199. During the period 1946-49 a total of 422 machines were built by Avia, and Letov added 129 to this figure. Until the early 1950s this Bf 109 development formed the backbone of the Cz.A.F. fighter squadrons. The Avia factory also produced the first jets, a batch of ten Me 262 fighters; seven were Me 262A models, and three were two-seat Me 262Bs. This small series was produced in

1947, and used for the training of the first Czech jet fighter pilots, remaining in service until 1954; one of each model is preserved in the National Technical Museum and the Air Museum in Prague. Avia also delivered to the Cz.A.F. its first helicopters—two Focke-Achgelis Fa 223 Drachen, built in 1947 and used by both the Air Force and the Air Guard. Many other types were used singly or in small numbers, including three Heinkel 219 Uhu; some Ju 52/3m and Ju W.34; 14 Klemm K1 35; and examples of the He 72D, Fw 44, Go 145, Ar 66, Fw 190A and Fw 190D, Siebel Fh 104, Bf 108, Fw 58, Piper Cub, and Heinkel He 111—one of which served in a photographic capacity as late at 1958. Twelve B-24 Liberators were acquired in exchange for 26 Mosquito F.B.VIs.

In 1948 a batch of 25 Czech-built Bf 109s were sold to the Israelis, as well as most of the surviving Czech Spitfires; the Cold War had brought with it embargoes which denied the Cz.A.F. ammunition for the Spitfires' guns. With the Mosquitos this problem was partly overcome by changing some of the guns for German weapons. In the early 1950s the need for ground-attack aircraft became increasingly acute, and the assault units were gradually equipped with heavily-armed Ilyushin I1-10 aircraft manufactured under licence by Avia at Prague; a total of 1,200 were built, including two-seat trainers. The basic decision to equip the post-war Cz.A.F. with mainly Soviet types had in fact been taken before the end of the war; this was one of the points of the so-called Košice Government Programme which was followed consistently as late as the early 1950s. Almost all German equipment was replaced by Soviet designs; the Bf 109 by the Yak-23 and MiG-15, the Arado Ar 96B by the Yak-11, the Mosquito by the Il-28, the Li-2 and Douglas C-47 by the Il-12 and Il-14, and the trainers by indigenous designs; the Bückers gave way to the Zlin-126, and the Fi 156 to the L-60 Brigadyr. The equipment of the combat regiments was progressively modernised, comprising at various times the MiG-15, MiG-15bis, MiG-17, MiG-19, and MiG-21. The ground attack Ilyushin I1-10s were replaced by MiG-15s and later by Sukhoi Su-7s. The Aero Ae-45, L-200 Morava and Antonov An-2 were introduced for liaison and light transport duties, together with Mi-1, Mi-4 and Mi-8 helicopters.

The Czechoslovak Air Force is now a member of the Warsaw Pact forces, and, naturally, no details are released for publication.

Aircraft Camouflage and Markings

As in all air forces, the colour schemes and markings of Cz.A.F. machines have altered considerably down the years. During the first two years of the force's existence no camouflage scheme was introduced; aircraft retained the original camouflage of their country of origin— Austro-Hungarian, French, or Russian. The first official national marking was a red-blue-white roundel, marked above and below the wing tips and on the fin and rudder. Anatra biplanes also bore this roundel on the fuselage sides. The roundel, which was sometimes additionally outlined in white, was very similar to the Imperial Russian marking.

In 1920 a new national marking was introduced. This was a red-white-blue flag above and below the wing tips and on both sides of the fin and rudder, positioned so that the white field was always outboard on the wings, and above the red field on the tail. The first Czech camouflage scheme was introduced at this time; upper surfaces were finished in a pattern of dark earth, tan and dark green, while undersurfaces were painted silver. The type designation and serial were painted in black on the sides of the engine cowling. In certain cases, e.g. the Letov Šm-1, the characters were "shadowed". Three regimental badges were brought into use on 1 January 1924; the 1st Air Regiment used a black Czech lion on a white field; the 2nd Air Regiment, a black Moravian eagle on a white field; and the 3rd Air Regiment, a black Slovakian cross over three hills, on a white field. These badges were painted on each side of the fuselage, and the dimensions were roughly 50cm. × 45cm. Outstanding

Above: Letov S-20 fighter powered with a Skoda HS 8Fb engine of 300h.p., of the 2nd Air Regiment, Olomouc. 95 were delivered to the Cz.A.F. and a small series to the Lithuanian A.F.

Above: Letov S-20 of the 2nd Air Regiment on Olomouc airfield, 1928.

Below: Line-up of Letov S-20's, 2nd Air Regiment, note the squadron codes which were introduced in 1931. 36th Squadron aircraft

Above: Fokker D-VII of Austro-Hungarian origin on the airfield at Olomouc, 1922.
Below: Breguet Br.14, one of ten delivered from France during 1919–20.

Below: Breguet Br.14 after a landing incident near the village of Majetin some time in 1924.

service by individuals, crews or units was marked by permission to paint the background of the regimental badge in scarlet. This permission was given by the Minister of National Defence, and applied only for one year. At this time it became standard practice to paint training aircraft silver overall.

In 1926 two important innovations were made. All aircraft except trainers were now painted in khaki-green on upper surfaces and silver on undersurfaces. The old flag-type national markings was replaced by a circle with equal red-white-blue segments; the circle was initially outlined in blue, but after 1933 it sometimes appeared with a red edge. Again, the white segments were always painted outboard. This colour scheme remained in use until 1939. In 1931, after the other three air regiments were established, new badges were introduced as follows: 1st A.R., white Czech lion on blue field; 2nd A.R., blue Moravian eagle on white field; 3rd A.R., red Slovakian cross on white field; 4th A.R., blue Czech lion on white field; 5th A.R., red Moravian eagle on white field; 6th A.R., red Czech lion on white field.

From 1931 onwards squadron code letters and numerals were introduced and painted on both sides of the fuselage. If the surface was khaki, the letters were painted in white; if the surface was silver or light blue, the markings were in blue. The code letters C and S were reserved for the Central Flying School and the Aviation Research Institute respectively. The temporary painting of large black or white numerals above and below the wings was common during Army and Air Force manoeuvres.

Shortly after the occupation of March 1939, an unusual marking appeared on machines at the Prague-Letnany base; this comprised a black swastika on the fin and rudder, and also above and below the wings. This marking

Gordou-Leseurre B-3 a small number of these high wing parasol monoplanes were operated by the Cz.A.F. during the 1920's. Photograph was taken on Cheb airfield about 1927.

was observed on Avia B-71s, Letov Š-50s, Aero A-101s and Avia 122s.

The only operations conducted by the Cz.A.F. over home territory during the Second World War were those of the Slovak National Uprising. The usual marking on insurgent aircraft, particularly the "Combined Squadron", comprised the Cz.A.F. circle with a white Slovak cross on the blue segment, above a black undulating line (see illustrations).

The immediate post-war scheme consisted of dark green upper surfaces and pale blue undersides; trainers were finished in light grey or silver. The national marking remained in the pre-war style, outlined in white on dark green surfaces and in insignia blue on pale blue surfaces. Code letters and numerals on fuselage sides were in white, and in black under the wings. All trainers carried black codes. An additional marking for trainer aircraft was introduced in the early 1950s, comprising a yellow stripe on the upper wing and fuselage surface—see illustration of the C-105. A distinct marking was carried by aircraft of the Air Guard, or "Air Police", in both pre-war and post-war periods. The cowlings, wing leading edges and undersurfaces were painted red, and the civil-style registration, OK-BYH, was painted in red letters outlined in white. The national marking was in the shape of an equal-curve triangle, and appeared on the fin and rudder only. The Air Guard used, at one time or another, the Dewoitine D-2, Avia B-534, Letov Š-218, Bf 109G, S-199, Arado Ar 96B, Fi 156, La-5, and Fh 204.

The camouflage of aircraft of British and Soviet origin, such as the Spitfire, Mosquito, Lavochkin La-5 and La-7, Pe-2 and Il-2, remained in its original state; however, there were a few exceptions, such as Squadron Leader Pošta's silver Spitfire with red lightning-flash markings. As time wore on, and camouflage was retouched with available stocks of paint, the upper surface shades naturally tended to differ slightly. The present Cz.A.F. jet equipment is almost entirely in natural metal finish, and code letter and numeral combinations were replaced in the late 1950s by numerals only. A few regimental badges were introduced in 1968, and are illustrated on the accompanying pages.

In late 1945 a code of aircraft designations was introduced and used up to 1958, when the original type designations were reintroduced.

Table of Czech A.F. aircraft designations

Fighter aircraft:

S-89	Supermarine Spitfire L.F.IXE
S-90	Focke-Wulf FW-190A
S-92	Messerschmitt Me-262A
S-95	Lavochkin La-5FN
S-97	Lavochkin La-7
S-99	Messerschmitt Bf-109G-6
S-199	Avia built Bf-109 with Jumo
S-100	Yakovlev Yak-17
S-101	Yakovlev Yak-23
S-102	MiG-15

Light bombers:

LB-36	D.H. Mosquito with German m.g.
LB-77	Heinkel He-111H
LB-79	Heinkel He-219 Uhu

Attack aircraft:

B-31	Ilyushin Il-2
B-32	Petlyakov Pe-2FT
B-36	D.H. Mosquito Mk.VI
B-37	Junkers Ju-87D

Transport aircraft:

D-41	Avro Anson
D-42	Airspeed Oxford
D-44	Siebel Fh-204D
D-47	Douglas C-47
D-52	Junkers Ju-52/3m
D-54	Siebel Fh-104
D-58	Focke-Wulf FW-58

Liaison aircraft:

K-61	Taylorcraft Auster
K-62	Polykarpov Po-2
K-65	Fieseler Fi-156
K-68	Piper Cub
K-70	Messerschmitt Bf-108
K-73	Noorduin C-64A Norseman
K-74	Fairchild UC-61

Trainers:

C-1	Klemm Kl-35D
C-2	Arado Ar-96B
C-3	Siebel Fh-204D
C-4	Bücker Bü-131
C-104	Bu-131 with Walter engine
C-5	Zlin-126
C-105	Zlin-126 modified
C-6	Bücker Bü-181
C-106	Bu-181 modified
C-7	Zlin-22
C-8	Piper L-4
C-9	FW-44/ČKD built
C-10	Bf-109G-6
C-110	Bf-109G-12
C-12	He-72
C-14	FW-44/German built
C-15	Gotha Go-145
C-16	Arado Ar-66
C-19	Praga E-39
C-23	Morane MS-234
C-25	Beneš-Mráz Be-250
C-26	Arado Ar-396

Fighter-Trainers:

CS-92	Me-262B
CS-95	La-5FN-UTI
CS-99	Bf-109G-12
CS-199	Two-seat S-199
CS-102	MiG-15 UTI

Attack-Trainers:

CB-31	Ilyushin Il-2U
CB-32	Petlyakov Pe-2U

Gliders:

NK-1	WACO CG-4A
NK-14	Yakovlev Yak-14
NK-25	Cybin C-25

Helicopters:

VR-1	Focke-Achgelis 223
VR-2	HC-2
VR-3	Mi-1
VR-4	Mi-4

Letov S-1 designed by Alois Smelek this was the first type of pure Czech design to enter service with the Cz.A.F.

Above: Aero A-11 of the 1st Air Regiment on Kbely airfield, Prague in 1925, a total of one hundred and seven A-11's had been delivered by 1928.

Right: A pair of Aero A-12's of the 3rd Air Regiment in flight, note the camouflage pattern.

Below: Aero A-11 reconnaissance biplane, 3rd Air Regiment, Piestany airfield, Slovakia 1929.

Below: Letov S-16 reconnaissance bomber prototype.

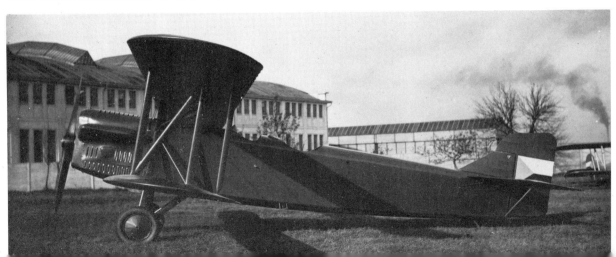

Above: Letov S-21 of the Central Flying School, Prostejov, the S-21 was a training version of the S-20 fighter.

Left: Letov S-31, 2nd Air Regiment, 36th Squadron after a forced landing in the Bohemian-Moravian Highlands in 1923.

Left: Letov S-31, serial No. 2 outside a hangar on Olomouc airfield, the Indian head was the personal insignia of Skpt. Kalla.

Below: Letov S-31 powered with a 480h.p. Walter Jupiter engine, thirty-two were delivered during 1932.

Letov S-6 bomber of 1923 powered by a Maybach Mb.IVa engine of 260h.p., 1st Air Regiment.

Avia BH-26 two-seat fighter of 1927 powered by a Walter Jupiter IV of 450h.p., 3rd Air Regiment, Nitra airfield, Slovakia.

Aero A-100 bomber, 1st Air Regiment, Prague, 1933. Powered by a 650h.p. Avia Vr-16 engine.

Below: Aero A-32 of the 3rd Air Regiment on Piestany airfield, 450 h.p. Walter Jupiter. Sixteen A-32's were delivered to the Finnish A.F., in 1929.

Above: Letov S-328 2nd Air Regiment note code and regimental insignia, photo taken on 22 June 1937.

Above: Close-up photo showing details of the insignia applied to Letov S-328's presented to the Cz.A.F., by the people of South Bohemia, note all lettering and surround are white applied directly to fuselage colour.

Above: Another Letov S-328 photographed after the mobilisation of 1938, note the code has been retained but the regimental badge has been overpainted.

Below: Letov S-328V target-tug seaplane.

Above: Nice flying shot of an Avia BH-21 in the markings of the Aviation Research Institute, Prague. 159 BH-21's were delivered to the Cz.A.F., and SABCA built a total of 50 under licence for the Belgian A.F.

Right: Avia BH-21 with Skoda HS 8 Fb 300h.p., engine, an excellent aerobatic aircraft, the pilot is Frantisek Novak.

Left: Rare flying shot of a Avia Ba-33 of the 3rd Regiment.

Below: Very good detail shot of an Avia Ba-33 with Skoda L of 500h.p. The majority of the fighter squadrons were equipped with the Ba-33 during the thirties.

Left: Aero A-100 of the 3rd Air Regiment flying over a village in Slovakia.

Below: Aero A-100's of the 1st Air Regiment on a formation training flight.

Above: Formation of Avia-Fokker F.IX's of the 5th Bomber Air Regiment, Brno.

Above: 5th Air Regiment Avia-Fokker F.IX taking off.

Below: Close-up of a Avia-Fokker F.IX of the 5th Air Regiment, Brno.

Right: Marcel Bloch MB.200 of the 5th Air Regiment from Brno, the photograph was taken after the mobilisation of 1938 when the regimental insignia was painted out and only the code retained. 124 MB.200's were built under licence by Avia and Aero during 1936–37.

Below: Letov S-50 reconnaissance bomber in prototype form only, tested during summer of 1938 by Cz.A.F. then by the Luftwaffe at Rechlin during 1939–40.

Above: Avia B-158 prototype.

Right: Aero A-300 bomber prototype of 1938, the last pre-war design of the Aero factory.

Below: Aero A-304 was a military version of the civil transport A-204, 15 were delivered during 1938. The letter S indicates this aircraft was under test by the Aviation Research Institute, Prague.

Above: Avia B-534 of early production batch, note radiator under cowl and open cockpit.

Above: Avia B-534 of the third production series with Avia HS 12Ydrs engine of 850h.p.

Above: Avia Bk-534, a cannon-armed version with the HS Ycrs 850h.p. engine.

Above: Avia B-534 of the fourth production batch before delivery to a squadron.

Below: A flight of Avia Bk-534's in the markings of the Slovak Air Force, flying over the Ukraine in 1941.

Below: An Avia B-534 dispersed on a Ukrainian airfield in 1941.

Above: Avia B-35 monoplane fighter of 1938.

Above: Avia B-135 prototype with retractable u/c, twelve were delivered to the Bulgarian A.F. in 1941.

Above: Praga E-51 reconnaissance prototype of 1938.

Above: Messerschmitt Bf.109E, 12th Squadron, Slovak A.F.

Above: Messerschmitt Bf.109E, 12th Squadron, Slovak A.F. flying over the River Vah. Note the position of the crosses and the absence of markings on the fin of both aircraft.

Below: Gotha Go.145A, Slovak A.F., on the airfield at Zvolen, 1943.

Below: Klemm Kl.35D, Slovak A.F., flying over Trencin.

23

Above: Heinkel He.111H, Slovak A.F. Note the blue cross with red disc tail marking, yellow fuselage band (and wing tips) and white code, standard Luftwaffe splinter scheme.

Above: Savoia Marchetti SM.84bis, Slovak A.F., note the original Italian markings on the rudders and white fuselage band.

Above: Focke-Wulf Fw.189, Slovak A.F.

Left: A dramatic photograph of the Slovak National Uprising. A part of the combined squadron, encircled by German troops, prepares to take off in October 1944. Note Fw.189 in Slovak Insurgent A.F., markings.

Left: Letov S-328 of the Combined Squadron on Tri Duby (Three Oaks) airfield. Note the Slovak Insurgent A.F. insignia.

Left: Slovak Insurgent A.F., Messerschmitt Bf.109G taxying on Tri Duby airfield, near Zvelu during the uprising of September 1944.

Cz.A.F., Supermarine Spitfire LF IXe's, 312th Fighter Squadron after their arrival from England at Prague-Ruzyn airport during the autumn of 1945.

Supermarine Spitfire LF IXe, 313th Fighter Squadron, serial SL657.

Spitfire LF IXe of the Central Flying School. Cz.A.F., designation of all Spitfires was S-98.

De Havilland Mosquito FB 6, Atlantic Squadron, code IY-12. Twenty-six were delivered as replacements for the Consolidated Liberators of 311th Squadron.

Mosquito FB 6, Atlantic Squadron, serial RF823. Cz.A.F., designation was B-36.

Below: Consolidated Liberator GR VI, 311th Bomber Squadron, note the original code letters of the wartime No. 311 Squadron, Coastal Command, RAF, serial KG859. Photo taken on Prague-Kbely airfield in 1945.

25

Above: Lavochkin La.5's of the 1st Czechoslovakian Fighter Regiment lined-up on Przeborsk airfield, 7 November 1944.

Another shot of La.5's of the same unit, inscription on the nose of nearest aircraft reads "Za svobodne Ceskoslovensko po boku Rude Armady" = "For Free Czechoslovakia beside the Red Army".

La.5's of the 1st Czechoslovakian Fighter Regiment, Przeborsk airfield, November 1944.

La.5 in post-war markings, code letters OP-13 in white on fuselage, in black under wings, red spinner. Malacky airfield, Slovakia.

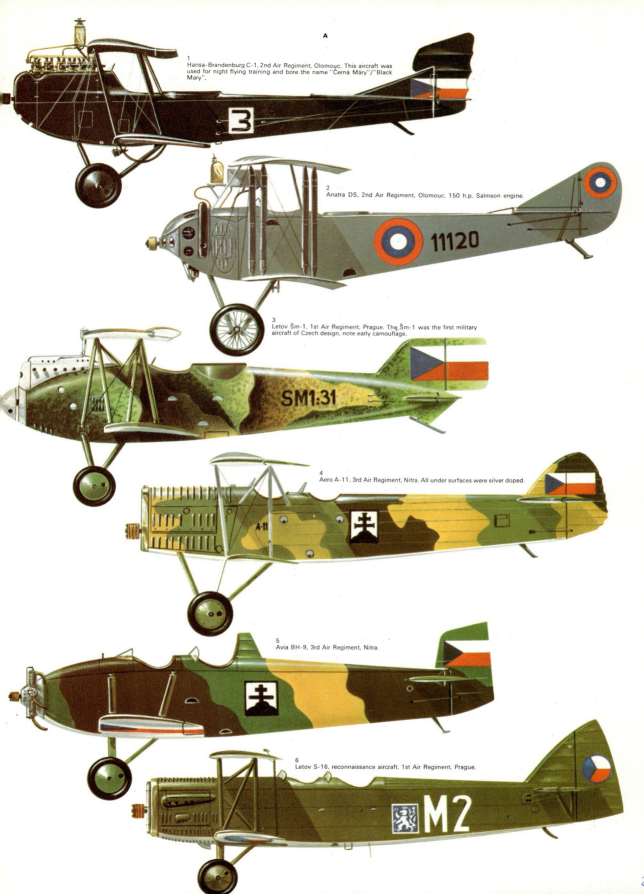

A

1
Hansa-Brandenburg C-1, 2nd Air Regiment, Olomouc. This aircraft was used for night flying training and bore the name "Černá Máry"/"Black Mary".

2
Anatra DS, 2nd Air Regiment, Olomouc. 150 h.p. Salmson engine.

3
Letov Šm-1, 1st Air Regiment, Prague. The Šm-1 was the first military aircraft of Czech design, note early camouflage.

4
Aero A-11, 3rd Air Regiment, Nitra. All under surfaces were silver doped.

5
Avia BH-9, 3rd Air Regiment, Nitra.

6
Letov S-16, reconnaissance aircraft, 1st Air Regiment, Prague.

B

1
Aero A-18, 2nd Air Regiment, Olomouc.

2
Letov Š-20, 2nd Air Regiment, Olomouc.

3
Avia BH-21, 3rd Air Regiment, Nitra. Note the early
black and white regimental insignia.

4
Avia Ba-33, 3rd Air Regiment, Piestany.

5
Letov Š-231, 2nd Air Regiment, Olomouc.

6
Avia B-534, 13th Squadron, Slovak Air Force, Eastern Front, Kiev
sector, early 1942.

C

1
Letov Š-328, 6th Air Regiment, Milovice. Š-328's were
nicknamed "Kravka" (Small Cow).

MĚSTO
ČESKÉ BUDĚJOVICE
JIŽNÍ CECHY ARMÁDĚ

2
Aero A-100, Central Flying School, Prostějov.

3
Aero A-42, one of two bomber prototypes built.

4
Aero A-300, bomber prototype, Aviation Research Institute,
Prague.

5
Aero MB-200, 5th Air Regiment, Brno. Marcel Bloch
built under licence.

6
Avia F-IX, 5th Air Regiment, Brno. Fokker F-IX built
under licence.

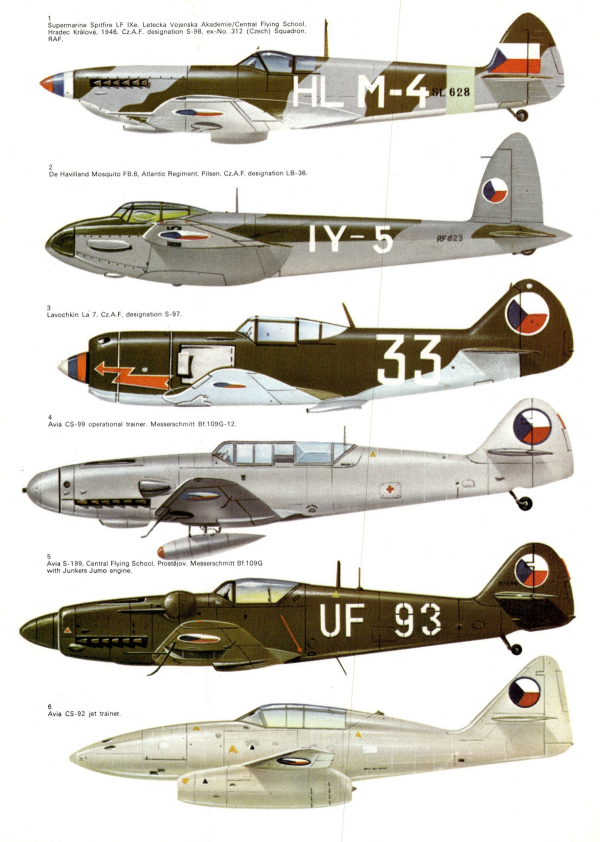

D

1
Supermarine Spitfire LF IXe, Letecka Vojenska Akademie/Central Flying School, Hradec Králové, 1946. Cz.A.F. designation S-98, ex-No. 312 (Czech) Squadron, RAF.

2
De Havilland Mosquito FB.6, Atlantic Regiment, Pilsen. Cz.A.F. designation LB-36.

3
Lavochkin La 7. Cz.A.F. designation S-97.

4
Avia CS-99 operational trainer. Messerschmitt Bf.109G-12.

5
Avia S-199, Central Flying School, Prostějov. Messerschmitt Bf.109G with Junkers Jumo engine.

6
Avia CS-92 jet trainer.

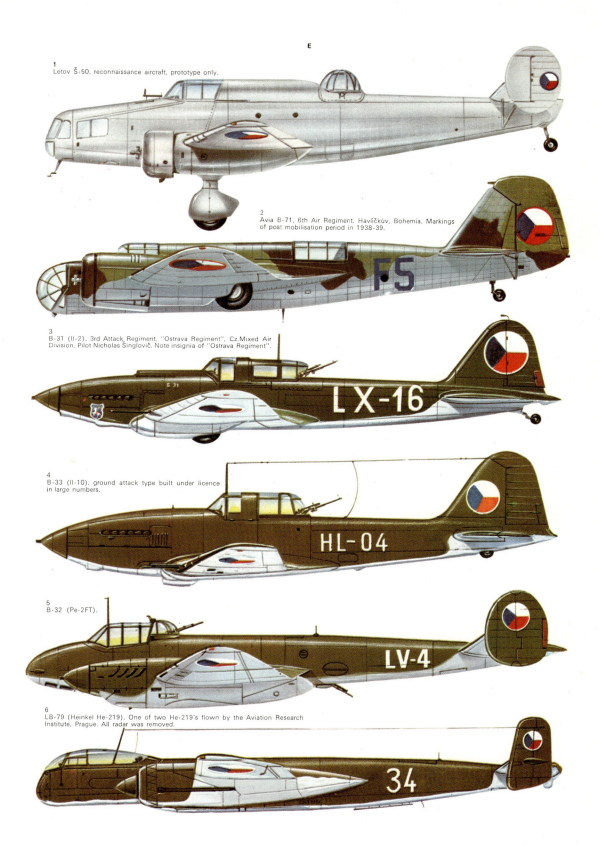

E

1
Letov Š-50, reconnaissance aircraft, prototype only.

2
Avia B-71, 6th Air Regiment, Havlíčkův, Bohemia. Markings of post mobilisation period in 1938-39.

3
B-31 (Il-2), 3rd Attack Regiment, "Ostrava Regiment", Cz.Mixed Air Division. Pilot Nicholas Šinglovič. Note insignia of "Ostrava Regiment".

4
B-33 (Il-10), ground attack type built under licence in large numbers.

5
B-32 (Pe-2FT).

6
LB-79 (Heinkel He-219). One of two He-219's flown by the Aviation Research Institute, Prague. All radar was removed.

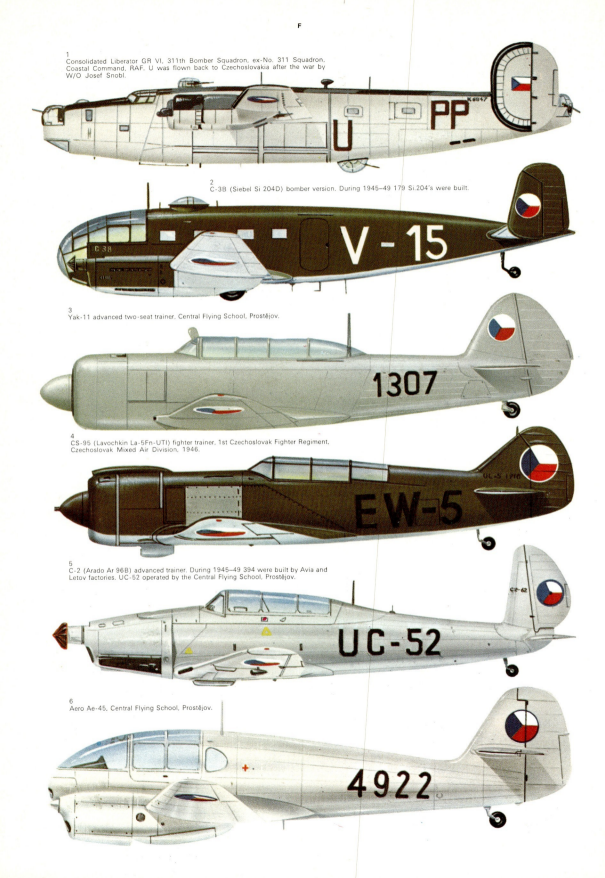

1 Consolidated Liberator GR VI, 311th Bomber Squadron, ex-No. 311 Squadron, Coastal Command, RAF. U was flown back to Czechoslovakia after the war by W/O Josef Snobl.

2 C-3B (Siebel Si 204D) bomber version. During 1945–49 179 Si.204's were built.

3 Yak-11 advanced two-seat trainer, Central Flying School, Prostějov.

4 CS-95 (Lavochkin La-5Fn-UTI) fighter trainer, 1st Czechoslovak Fighter Regiment, Czechoslovak Mixed Air Division, 1946.

5 C-2 (Arado Ar 96B) advanced trainer. During 1945–49 394 were built by Avia and Letov factories. UC-52 operated by the Central Flying School, Prostějov.

6 Aero Ae-45, Central Flying School, Prostějov.

1
Yak-17, the first Soviet jet aircraft type delivered to the Cz.A.F.

2
Yak-23 operational trainer.

3
MiG-15, most important fighter of the 50's in the Cz.A.F.

4
MiG-19, first supersonic fighter of the Cz.A.F.

5
MiG-21, first line fighter of the Cz.A.F.

6
Sukhoi Su-7BM, multi-purpose attack aircraft.

Preylowski

1
Zlin Z-26 Trener, elementary two-seat trainer, Central Flying School, Prostějov.

2
SPP L-200A Morava, light transport and liasion aircraft.

3
L-29 Delfin jet trainer. First jet aircraft of Czech design.

4
MiG-15-UTI jet trainer.

5
Ilyushin Il-28.

6
Avia B-35 fighter prototype in 1938 period camouflage.

Right: Petlyakov Pe.2, Cz.A.F., designation B-32, a small number were operated during the immediate post-war years.

Right: Ilyushin Il.2, "Ostrava" Regiment, code LX-16 in white.

Below: Ilyushin Il.2, Cz.A.F., designation B-31, serial on cowl B 31-18894113, "Ostrava" Regiment, note the regimental insignia on cowl.

Above: C-2 (Arado Ar.96B) trainer. Note camera-gun pod beneath front cockpit. 394 C-2's were built by Avia and Letov factories during 1945—49.

Above: C-4 (Bucker Bu.131) elementary trainer. Military Air Academy, Hradec Kralove.

Above: C-2 (Ar.96B) advanced trainer, Aviation Research Institute, Prague.

Below: C-6 (Bu.181) elementary trainer, Flying School, Prostejov.

Above: D-58 (Focke-Wulf Fw.58 Weihe) of German origin.

Above: D-4 (Siebel Fh.104), personal aircraft of General A. Vicheret, Chief of the Cz.A.F., 1945–48.

Right: D-52 (Junkers Ju.52-3m) transport, painted overall dark green with white cheat line and code.

Below: LB-77 (Heinkel He.111H). This LB-77 was used for photographic duties, delivered from Bulgaria in 1945 it was still flying in 1956. Note absence of belly gun-positions.

Below: C-3A (Siebel Si.204D) used for navigational training. During 1945–49 Aero and Praga built 179 examples.

elow: K-65 (Fieseler Fi.156 Storch). Aviation Research Institute, rague. 138 built by Mraz.

Below: VR-1 (Focke-Achgelis Fa. 223 Drachen). First helicopters of the Cz.A.F.

Left: S-199 (Bf.109G). A total of 422 were built by Avia during 1946–49 and 129 by Letov during 1948–49, all with the Junkers Jumo 211F engine.

Below: S-199 fighters guarded the West frontier of Czechoslovakia during the late forties and early fifties.

Below: CS-99 (Bf.109G-12) in overall silver finish.

Below left: CS-199 (Bf.109G-12 with Jumo 211F). Photo taken at Celechovice near Prostejov, July 1956.

Above right, below left and right: S-92 (Messerschmitt Me.262B), the first jet aircraft in the Cz.A.F.

Top: B-33 (Ilyushin Il-10) ground attack aircraft were built under licence by Avia, during 1952—55 about 1200 were built.

Above: Nice three-quarter rear shot of a B-33.

Below: Two fine flying shots of CB-33 trainers, note the modified rear cockpit and the very neat paint job.

39

Left: S-100 (Yakovlev Yak-1[?]) was the first Soviet jet fighter [in?] Cz.A.F. One example only w[as?] tested and is shown here af[ter?] renovation in the Aviati[on] Museum on Prague-Kbe[ly] airfield.

Left: S-101 (Yakovlev Yak-2[3]) jet fighters were, with t[he] MiG-15 the first jets to ent[er] Cz.A.F. service.

Above: S-102 (MiG-15) with RD-45F engine built under licence.   Below: S-102 rolling down the taxi strip on an operational airfield.

Above: CS-102 (MiG-15UTI) two-seat fighter-trainer, the black 34 on the nose is a factory and not a service designation.

Above: MiG-17 with drop tanks and below, note radome details.

Above: Line-up of MiG-19's on a Cz.A.F. base, the first supersonic jet fighter in service.

Above: Good close-up shot of a MiG-19.   Below: MiG-21 being re-fuelled and re-armed.

Above: Nice flying shot of a MiG-21, in actual fact flying high over the Tatra Mountains.

Above & below: The latest jet equipment of the Cz.A.F., the Sukhoi Su-7 attack fighter.

Left: C-5 (Zlin 26) elementary trainer was a replacement for the C-4 and C-6. During 1949–50 a total of 113 C-5's were delivered to the Cz.A.F.

Above: Ilyushin Il-14, alias Avia Av-14T transport, natural metal finish.

Above: C-11 (Yak-11) advanced trainer with ASh-21 700h.p. engine built under licence by SPP Kunovice.

Above: L-200A Morava, five seat light communications and transport aircraft, Otrokovice airfield, 15 September 1963.

Above: Lisunov Li.2 transport, known by many other names and designations, on the Prague-Kelby airfield, October 1968.

Above: K-75 (Aero Ae.45) light transport in light grey finish.

Below: Ilyushin Il-28 bomber.

Above: Ilyushin Il-28U bomber trainer.

Above & right: L-29 Delfin trainer, first flown on 5 August 1959, the first all Czech designed and built jet aircraft, built in large series and in many versions for many Air Forces.

Below: Antonov An-2 multi-purpose biplane.

Right: A pair of An-2's, nick-named "Andula" by pilots.

Below: Vr-2, alias HC-2 were the first home built helicopters in the Cz.A.F.

Below: Milj Mi-4 helicopters on Otrokovice airfield during 1963, they form the equipment of the helicopter regiments.

45

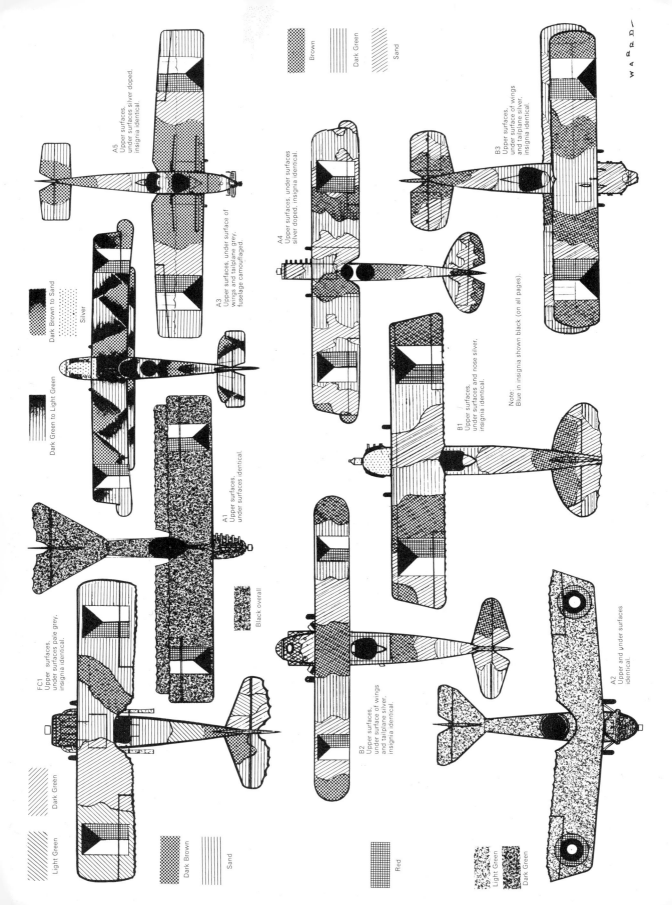

Brown

Dark Green

Sand

WARD

A5
Upper surfaces,
under surfaces silver doped,
insignia identical.

A3
Upper surfaces, under surface of
wings and tailplane grey,
fuselage camouflaged.

B3
Upper surfaces,
under surface of wings
and tailplane silver,
insignia identical.

A4
Upper surfaces, under surfaces
silver doped, insignia identical.

Dark Brown to Sand

Silver

Dark Green to Light Green

A1
Upper surfaces,
under surfaces identical.

B1
Upper surfaces,
under surfaces and nose silver,
insignia identical.

Note:
Blue in insignia shown black (on all pages).

FC1
Upper surfaces,
under surfaces pale grey,
insignia identical.

Black overall

B2
Upper surface of wings
and tailplane silver,
insignia identical.

A2
Upper and under surfaces
identical.

Light Green

Dark Green

Dark Brown

Sand

Red

Light Green

Dark Green

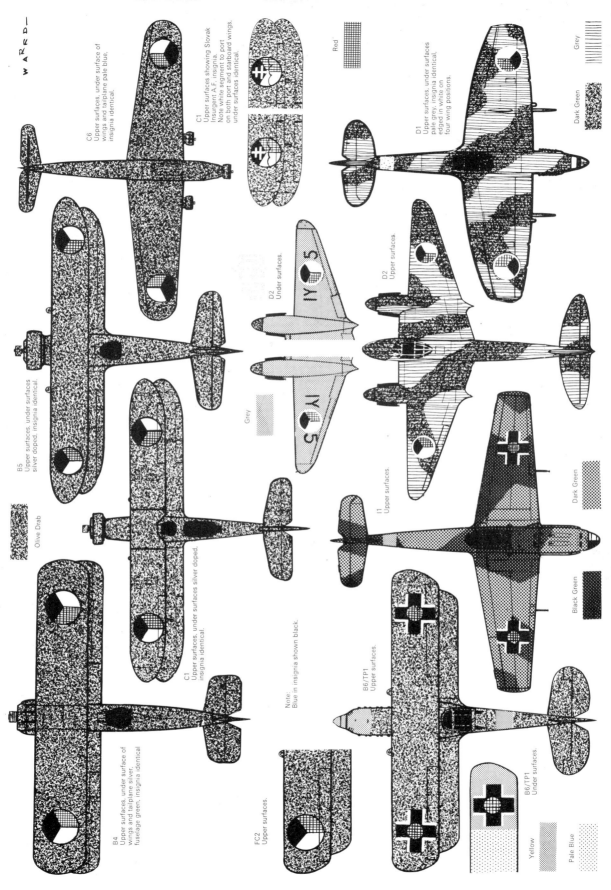

WARRD

C6
Upper surfaces, under surface of wings and tailplane pale blue, insignia identical.

C1
Upper surfaces showing Slovak Insurgent A.F. insignia. Note white segment to port on both port and starboard wings, under surfaces identical.

Red

D1
Upper surfaces, under surfaces pale grey, insignia identical, edged in white on four wing positions.

Grey

Dark Green

D2
Under surfaces.

D2
Upper surfaces.

B5
Upper surfaces, under surfaces silver doped, insignia identical.

Grey

I1
Upper surfaces.

Olive Drab

C1
Upper surfaces, under surfaces silver doped, insignia identical.

Dark Green

Black Green

Note:
Blue in insignia shown black.

B6/TP1
Upper surfaces.

B4
Upper surfaces, under surface of wings and tailplane silver, fuselage green, insignia identical.

FC2
Upper surfaces.

B6/TP1
Under surfaces.

Yellow

Pale Blue

47

W A R R D

E5
Upper surfaces,
under surfaces pale blue.
insignia identical.

E6
Upper surfaces,
under surfaces pale blue.
insignia identical.

Olive Green

E3
Upper surfaces pale blue,
under surfaces pale blue.
insignia identical.

F4
Upper surfaces,
under surfaces pale blue.
insignia identical.

Grey

Green

E4
Upper surfaces,
under surfaces pale blue.
insignia identical.

F1
Upper surfaces

Red

E2
Upper surfaces, under surfaces
pale blue/grey, insignia
identical. Red surround to
insignia in all positions.

Dark Earth

Grey/Green

Dark Green

D5
Upper and under surfaces identical.
White surround to insignia
in all positions.

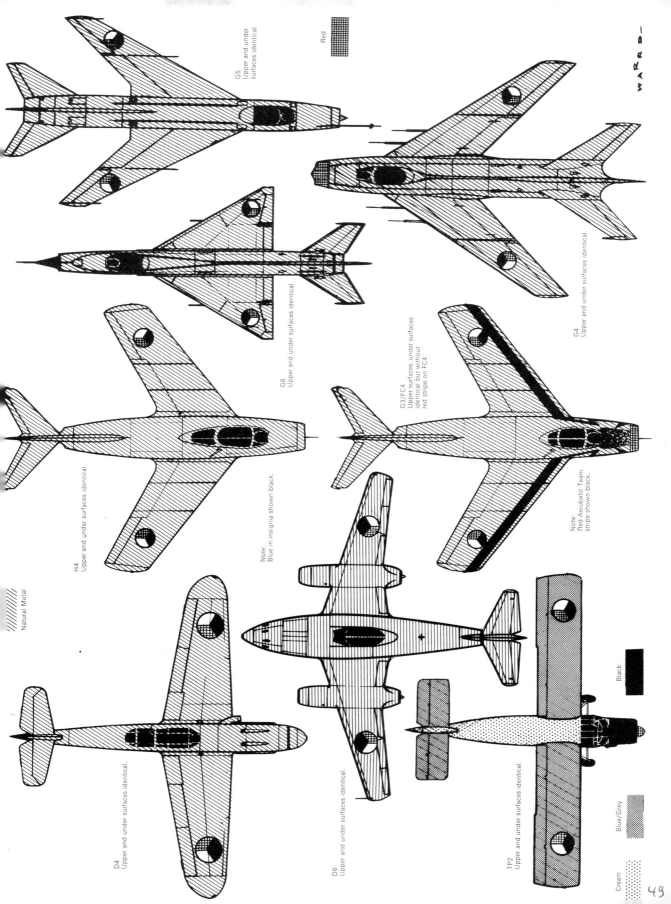

G5
Upper and under
surfaces identical.

Red

WARBI

G6
Upper and under surfaces identical.

G4
Upper and under surfaces identical.

G3/FC4
Upper surfaces, under surfaces
identical but without
red stripe on FC4.

Note:
Red Aerobatic Team
stripe shown black.

H4
Upper and under surfaces identical.

Note:
Blue in insignia shown black.

Natural Metal

D4
Upper and under surfaces identical.

D6
Upper and under surfaces identical.

TP2
Upper and under surfaces identical.

Black

Cream

Blue/Grey

49

Dark Earth

Grey/Green

Dark Green

H5
Upper and under surfaces identical.

H6
Upper surfaces, under surfaces
pale grey, insignia identical.

F5
Upper surfaces.

F5
Under surfaces,
port and starboard.

UC–52

G2
Upper and under surfaces identical.

H3
Upper and under surfaces identical.

F6
Upper and under surfaces identical.

Note:
Blue in insignia shown black.

Natural Metal

G1
Upper surfaces, under surfaces
pale blue, insignia identical.

Olive Green

H2
Upper and under surfaces identical.

Medium Blue